DATE DUE

listen
with
the
eye

listen with the eye

poems by
samuel hazo

photographs by
james p. blair

published by
university of
pittsburgh press

pittsburgh
pennsylvania

the motive

Animals
bore
me,
and angels
I would find
too perfect
to be suitable
for praise.

Considering
the best
and worst of men
and that the worst
alone
could dare
a saviour
to the earth,
I owe
a debt
to God
to praise
no creature
other than my
kind
before the best
of all the rest.

listen with the eye

Rapt,
a brother and his sisters
watch
what makes them
perfectly
themselves.
Profiled to me,
they see a clash
of quiet
in the air.

Backdrop:
a stucco wall,
a ridge
of concrete blocks—
unpainted.

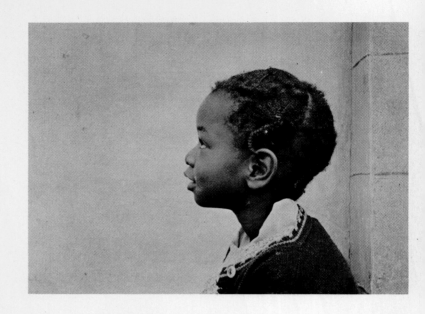

I think
of pantomimes,
tableaux
or dramas
free of props
and furthered only
by the hatch
and stay
of life
assumed
and held
illusory as fog
before the vanishing.

I seek no
further
metaphor
to speak my love
of children in the sun
in these eternal
Alabamas
of my mind.
It is enough that I can
think
I see them
there
like cameos,
and
there
they
are.

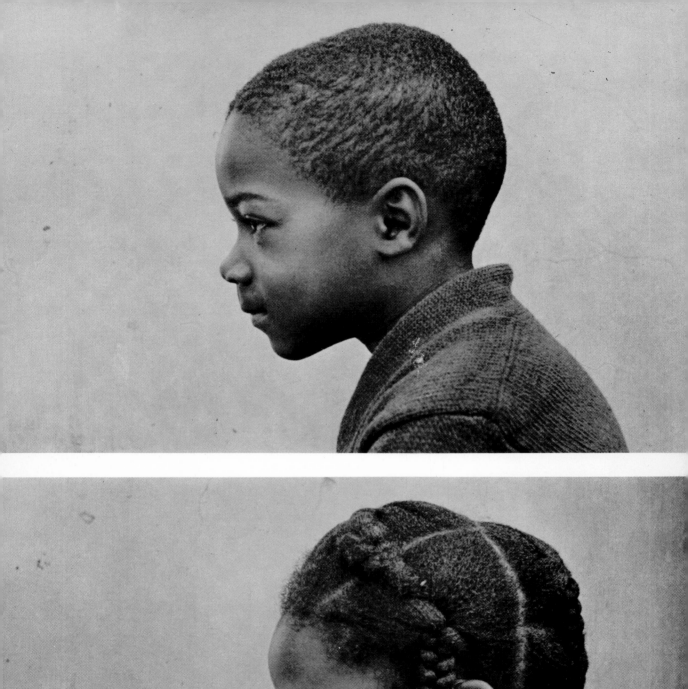

mother with child

What gathers at her heartbeat to recall

the ninth and longest month when she woke numb

with hurt and gathered in a satchel all

she needed for the trip and life to come?

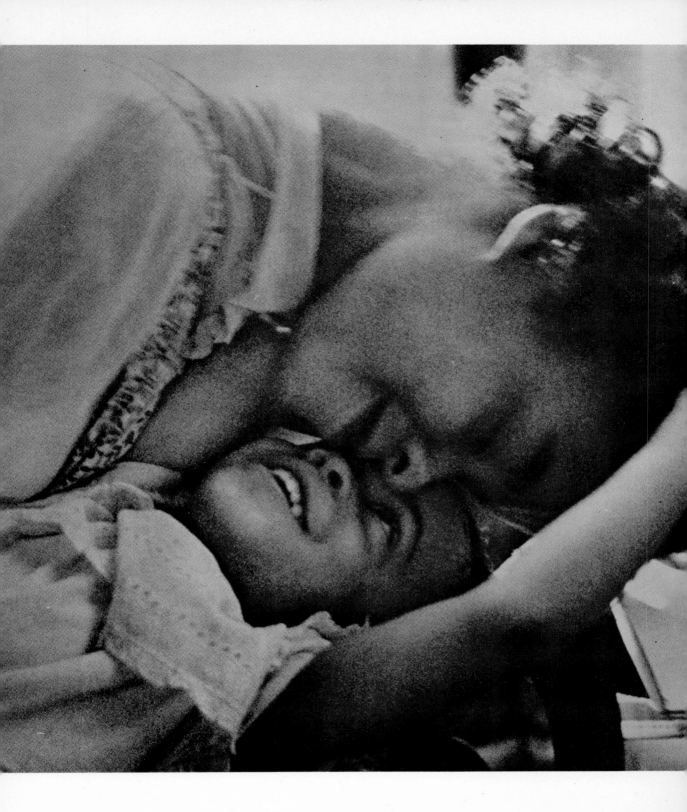

the pausers

A cabbie
leans
against a pole
and lets himself
turn mirror to the traffic
and the town.
A cripple,
squatting
on his crutches,
watches
me
until I am not there
to him
at all.

Stopping
and being stopped
are not the same.
Stopped,
we grimace
like a woman vexed
because her bus is
late.
Stopping,
we are two men
braced
against a bar.
We let our bodies
slacken
into sleep
and lend the money
of our thoughts
to one another
slowly
and without an
I. O. U.

A sleeper
in a rowboat
spells
the same
amen.
He boats his oars,
then lies
spreadeagled
in the bow
and closes
both his eyes
and lets
the rowboat
go.

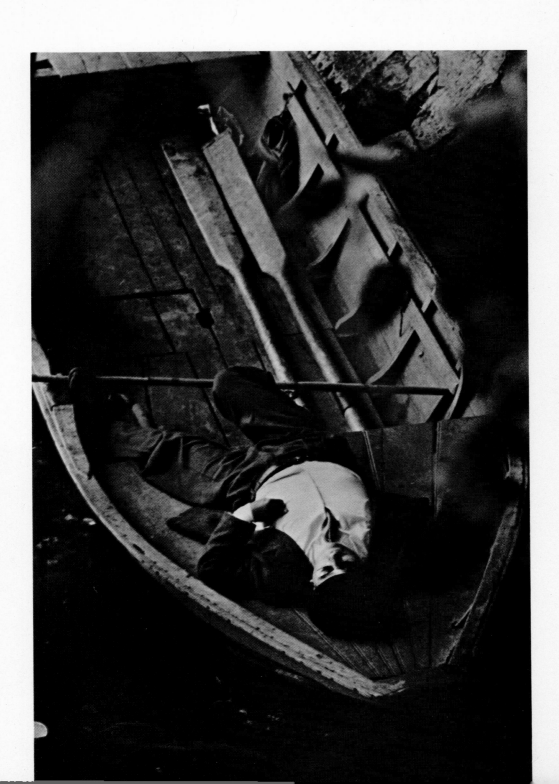

the yellow faces

Their eyes have never
changed.

They lead me
back
to centuries
before the youngest caesars
and the oldest pharaohs
fell.

Through them
I know a time of
khans,
Confucius,
coolies,
sampans,
water buffalo,
and gardens
neat as lace.

And still
their captive,
I return
like Marco Polo,
saying
I have seen
the dynasties,
the spools of silk,
the junks,
the land behind
the wall,
the fans
more delicately
painted
than the wings
of precious
moths.

I have glimpsed
Cathay
in Chinese eyes.

floozy

Turn us from eyes
that lack all light
like lanternflames
extinguished
by a puff
with hooking wicks
still stubbornly aglow
before the upward
burning
out,
from arms
abandoned on a lap,
from one black slouch
and silhouette
that cocks a bottle to the sky
where cables sway with sparrows,
and a clothesline sags
with torn pajamas
and a T-stitched sheet.

Turn us from someone on a step
before a hall
that funnels back
to radios turned on to jazz,
a purse upended
on a desk
for dimes,
a room wallpapered once
and never cleaned,
a Sunday comic section
spilled
across a sagging davenport.

Outside,
while trolleys rattle
on the rails
toward tomorrow's
promises,
what is this loneliness
in flesh
that makes us turn to find
her eyes,
and shrug,
and shake heads no,
and walk away
into
remembering?

harlequinade

Topple
from his stilts
the somersaulting dwarf,
caper to laughter,
twonk
for popcorn kids
your punchinello nose
or broom away
the pool of light
that tracks
your trampolining leaps
and falls
around the sawdust ring.

Let crowds
applaud
the first
of seven lions
whipped and chaired
through seven hoops
of flame,
or cheer
the tamer,
juggler,
death-defier,
acrobat,
 equestrian,
and cycling chimpanzee.
I glory
in the everlasting bum
and bide the boring skits
until his final pantomimes
as I have bided
sleek and Dieseled
freights
to see at last
the joggled
Toonerville caboose.

Rabbled down the bleachers,
nudged toward the exit flaps,
I turn to glimpse
a gang of clowns
undo suspendered pantaloons,
detach their lightbulb
noses,
towel off their Ringling grins
and slam a wad
of trappings
into circus trunks.
Lids drop shut.
Just
like
that
the world comes back.

pixie

She tugs her sweater
up
and overhead
until it crackles
prickly
on her arms
emerging paralleled
from evenly
inverting sleeves.

Unbelted now,
her waist turns
supple
when she turns
to play canary
for me
while she runs.
The wind
is fresh
with August,
and the feather-raising
breezes
volley
cool
across her cheeks
in soft releases.

She lifts her arms
and lowers them
and lifts them
and lowers them
palms down
as faultlessly
as closing
wings.

no man's land

A boy in knickers hunches on his knees
to cock his trigger-thumb and aim and shoot
at galaxies of marbles in a ring.
He stuffs his winnings in a drawstring bag
like pearls or nuggets only friends can see

at night in hideout yards he christens France
or Africa where lionslayers meet
to climb for apples and the highest pears.
When I invade his sidewalk shores and feel
the echo underfoot of passing vans,

he hears a surge of tanks, falls soldier-prone
and blasts unseen bazookas at their treads.
Then truce, then time to lark or look at stars
before he teeters on the tightrope curbs
and leapfrogs all the bareback hydrants home.

flight

Behind them always is
the town
diminished in departure,
a mattress rolled
and forced
into a wagon bay,
and tousled boys
papoosed
to mothers
bent and hiking
for the hope of ports.

They congregate to watch
from quiet quays
while sailors turn the capstans,
and the derricked cables
creak with rising
and descending
cargoes
cradled in a net.

Before them always
ebb away the tides
like roads that lead
and lead
from wanderings
to wonderings
where refuge and the refugee
are one,
and home is only
what you hold
and
what you are.

laborers

After the drying of the nets
across the seawash decks
or after the stacking of spades
beside abandoned picks
with mud still clotted
on the blades
that black men
swung and sledged
into the rocky clay,
air tastes of balsam
in a cigarette,
and wind against
the face
assuages
like a kiss.

Men grin and rest
as if from soldiering
or victory
with wristblood
pulsing
deep and certain
in the cooling afterward
of strain.

So lounged
or stood akimbo
centuries before them
seamen,
whalers,
pioneers,
centurions,
and those known only
as a sandaled race
that sculptors left
profiled in stone
like naked jacks
beneath
the tetrahedral rock
that peaks
the pyramid
of Cheops
mummied at attention
in his tomb.

the first liberator

It is written in a letter in Latin
to the King of Spain from Admiral Columbus
that he landed at San Salvador,
Santa María de la Concepción, Fernandina,
Isabella, Española and Juana
on his first voyage from Palos.

It is added that on each of these islands
south of Cathay
he never saw a native clothed,
that fleet canoes propelled by seventy rowers
often tracked his ships, that native women
labored for their men, who had but one wife,
that all, except the Indians of Charis,
were liberal and loving, though timid,
sharing meat and provisions equally.
They were dark as plums but unashamed.
They hunted with spears whittled from cane
and shunned cannibalism and war.

Though his men bartered broken bottles
for the natives' pure gold and cotton,
Columbus called the king
of Navidad del Señor
his brother,
noting nonetheless that the king's land
and the land of all the islands
south of Cathay
seemed "admirably adapted for tillage,
pasture and habitation."
To safeguard which for "the holy faith of Christ"
Columbus built and garrisoned a fortress
fully armed, imploring that
"processions be made,
and sacred feasts be held,
and the temples be adorned with festive boughs . .
in the prospect of the salvation of the souls
of so many nations hitherto lost."

At the departure of the clothed, white sailors
from San Salvador, Santa María de la Concepción,
Fernandina, Isabella, Española and Juana,
the natives waded after them
and waved their black and naked arms
or held their plum-dark children high
to see
"beings of a celestial race"
who had already taken two men
and twenty women
by force

and would return.

memoir at checkpoint

I will tell you the worst thing,
without tricks, without poetry.

I was standing beside a bed
and trying to keep eggnog from spilling.
Propped against three pillows
and spitting in a folded front page
was someone I loved,
dying,
who never struck me with a hand
or word.
Death was starting already
to rattle in his lungs.
And there I was standing—standing
with this absolutely useless drink
and watching how hard his breathing
came
or would not come
and for God's sake trying
not to show I knew the worst
and knew that there was nothing
I could do
but watch.

But I have buried that, have left
my father in another country
many borders back and now must wait
for clearance in a queue of sullen men
while guards with bayonets slouch by,
and no one knows my name.

masks

Behind his vizard
the crusader may
have laughed
or cursed,
but no one saw,
and none but the crusader
knew.

From shielded soldiers
to the counterfaces
of the fattest tarts,
the curtain of a mask
closes
and stays
closed.

Through Hallowe'ens
of all the three-act world,
I wonder
at warriors,
witch-doctors,
clowns,
actors or sandblasters,
kids in two-holed sheets
and every painted
or pretended face that's false,
if there can be a stop
to what they make me
ask—

Who's there?
Who are you?
Let me see your
face.

marauders

Her fear of them they took as sport—
her curse and scream when they advanced
as warnings better stopped with rags
torn brusquely from the dress she wore

and wound into a muffling hood
to keep her whimpering unheard,
her eyes and desperate tears unseen
and nil to those who masked her dread

until—thief-stealthily and still—
they fled from what they fouled and hid,
wiped once what stained their bayonets
and loped wolf-low toward the hills.

there is no straight line

Everything is circles:
the spun top
of the world,
the night, the day,
the night again——
the corn
from seed
to stalk
to corn
to seed.

We go
where we were,
and roads
are the same
to our coming
and going.

There is spring
in snow,
and summer
in April,
and autumn
in the first zinnia,
and January
in the last.

Look deep enough,
walk far enough,
live long enough,
and you will
learn
how all things
turn
and merry-go-round
around the sun,
and
make
a
zero.

credits

Floozy, Harlequinade, Laborers,
Flight, and No Man's Land, are used
with permission from
The Quiet Wars by Samuel Hazo,
Sheed & Ward, 1962, and Marauders,
from **Discovery and Other Poems**
by Samuel Hazo, Sheed & Ward, 1959.

The book was designed by
Jerome J. Schuerger, Pittsburgh.

Printed in the United States of America by
Book Craftsmen Associates, Inc., New York